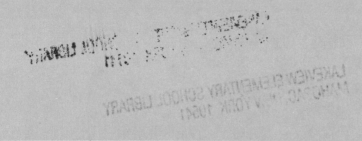

JONAH
AND THE
TWO GREAT FISH

MORDICAI GERSTEIN

SIMON & SCHUSTER BOOKS FOR YOUNG READERS

SIMON & SCHUSTER BOOKS FOR YOUNG READERS

An imprint of Simon & Schuster Children's Publishing Division

1230 Avenue of the Americas, New York, New York 10020

Copyright © 1997 by Mordicai Gerstein

All rights reserved including the right of reproduction in whole or in part in any form.

SIMON & SCHUSTER BOOKS FOR YOUNG READERS is a trademark of Simon & Schuster.

Book design by Lucille Chomowicz. The text for this book is set in 14--point Cochin.

Printed and bound in Hong Kong by South China Printing Co. (1988) Ltd.

First Edition 10 9 8 7 6 5 4 3 2 1

Library of Congress Cataloging-in-Publication Data

Gerstein, Mordicai.

   The legend of Jonah and the two great fish / Mordicai Gerstein.   p.   cm.

   Summary: Retells the Old Testament story of the man who disobeyed

God's wishes and was swallowed by a great fish.

   ISBN 0-689-81373-2 1. Jonah (Biblical prophet)—Juvenile literature.

2. Bible stories, English—O. T. Jonah. [1. Jonah (Biblical prophet)

2. Bible stories—O. T.] I. Title. BS1605.5.G37 1997 s224'.9209505—dc20 96-31971

The artwork was created with oil paint on vellum

For
Lou and Florence
with love

According to the Bible, there was once a prophet named Jonah.

A prophet is someone who speaks for God,

and sometimes foretells the future.

In the Jewish tradition many legends have arisen

about the characters and events in the Bible.

These legends fill in the gaps in the stories with all the details

that everyone wants to know:

what things and people really looked like,

exactly how much of something there was,

why something happened,

and what happened before and after.

Jonah was said to have been a disciple, or student,

of the prophet Elisha.

It is also told

that at what should have been the end of his life,

God allowed Jonah to enter Heaven and remain there alive!

Here, then, is the story of the prophet Jonah,

enriched by these legends.

It is told that Jonah was awakened one night by the voice of God.
"Jonah," said God, "you shall speak my words.
You will be my prophet.
Get up now and go to Ninevah, that great city. Tell the people
that forty days from now, because of their cruel and selfish ways,
I will destroy their city with earthquake, fire, and flood."

And Jonah thought, "God has made a mistake.
I am not ready to be a prophet.
I will forget what to say. I will stutter and the people will laugh at me."
Jonah hated being laughed at.

"I will run away," thought Jonah, "to where
God cannot find me.
I will go to sea."

"I will take a ship," thought Jonah,
"and sail to far Tarshish at the edge of the world."

But of course God saw Jonah and prepared a great storm.
The rest of the sea was calm, but the storm raged over Jonah's ship.
People of all nations were on the ship, and they were afraid.
Each prayed to a different god or goddess to save them.
But Jonah was sleeping and did not pray.

The people woke Jonah. "Why do you not pray?" they asked.
"Because," answered Jonah, "it is my God
who has sent the storm to punish me. I have disobeyed Him.
To save yourselves you must throw me into the sea."
"How can we believe you?" they cried.
"You must prove that you are the cause of the storm."

"Put my toes into the sea," said Jonah.

They touched Jonah's toes to the sea and the storm stopped.

They pulled Jonah's toes back, and again the storm raged.

"You see?" said Jonah. "Throw me into the sea."

And they did. In that instant the storm stopped.
The people were saved and the ship sailed away.

But Jonah sank to the bottom of the sea.
There, a great fish had been waiting
since the creation of the world to swallow him up.
"You must live in this fish, Jonah," said God,
"until you change your mind and do as I asked."

But to Jonah's surprise, the fish was spacious and well furnished inside.
There was a diamond that shone like the sun.
The fish's eyes were windows and through them
Jonah could see all the wonders of the deep.

For three days Jonah traveled under the sea
and enjoyed good food and many marvelous sights.
"Jonah is too comfortable," thought God.
"He will never change his mind and do as I asked."

So God sent another fish, much bigger than the first.
"Jonah must come with me," it said to the first fish,
"or I will swallow you both."

And the first fish gave Jonah up,
and the second fish swallowed him.

The second fish was a mother fish. Inside, it was dark and crowded
with thirty six thousand, five hundred baby fish of all kinds.

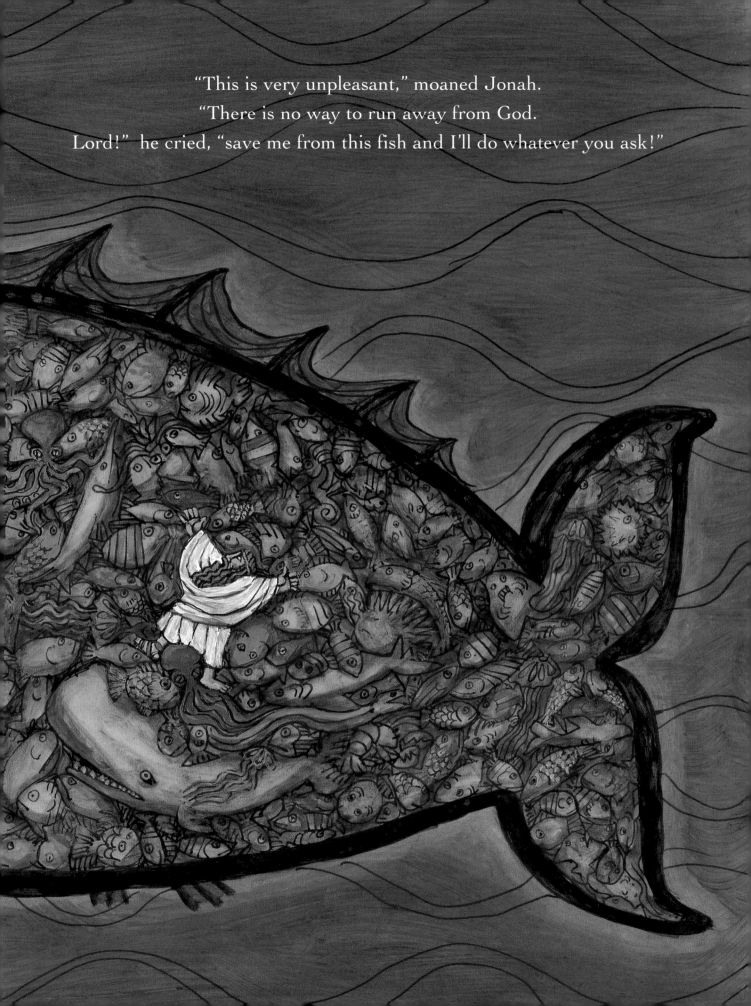

"This is very unpleasant," moaned Jonah.
"There is no way to run away from God.
Lord!" he cried, "save me from this fish and I'll do whatever you ask!"

God heard Jonah and said to the fish, "Release him."
And the fish opened her mouth and spat Jonah

nine hundred and sixty nine parasangs through the air to dry land.
"Thank you, Lord," said Jonah.

And Jonah did as God asked.
He went to Ninevah, that great city.

And Jonah said to the people of Ninevah,
"Forty days from now, because of your cruel and selfish ways,
God will destroy your city with earthquake, fire, and flood."
He did not stutter or forget what to say.

And the people listened to Jonah
and they were frightened.
They wept and asked
God to forgive them.
They became kind and generous,
loving and considerate.

Even the king of Ninevah wept
and gave all his gold to the poor.
And God saw that the people had changed.
He smiled and decided to forgive them.
He did not destroy their city.

And the people said to Jonah, "Look! Forty days have passed
and our city is not destroyed. You told us falsely!"

"Maybe God has forgiven you," said Jonah.

"You didn't say He would forgive us," they sneered.

"You said He would DESTROY US!

You are a FALSE PROPHET!" And they laughed at Jonah.

Jonah hated being laughed at.

Jonah ran into the desert and shouted to God,
"You see? You've made a fool of me!
Why did you not destroy them?"
And God asked Jonah,
"Are you right to be angry at me?"

Jonah did not answer. All day he sat sulking in the hot sun.
And God caused a beautiful gourd vine with
two hundred and seventy-five leaves to grow up
over Jonah and shade him.
"Ahhh," said Jonah. "Sweet vine, sweet shade."

But that night, God sent a worm to eat the roots of the vine.
The vine withered and died. And Jonah wept.
"God!" he wailed. "Why did you kill that beautiful vine
that gave me shade and shelter?"

And God said to Jonah,
"Look how you weep because I killed a little vine.
Think how much worse it would be to destroy a whole city
just because some foolish people laughed at you instead of thanking you.

Rejoice, Jonah! You have saved the one hundred
and twenty seven thousand people of Ninevah,
and all their sheep, goats, and cows that never hurt anyone. Rejoice!"

"Dear Lord," said Jonah, bowing his head.
"I *have* been a fool. Forgive me for my selfish anger.
I rejoice at being your messenger.
May the world be guided always by your goodness."

224
GER

Gerstein, Mordicai.

Jonah and the two
great fish.

$16.00

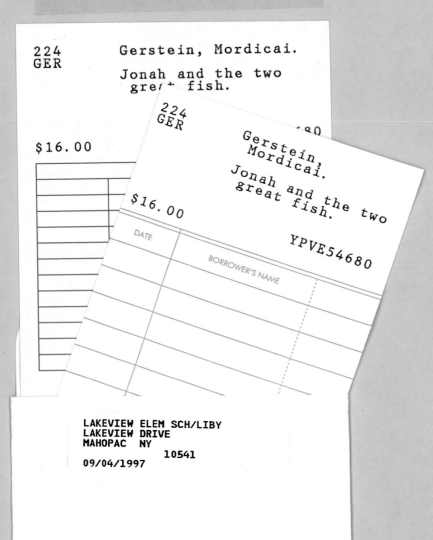

224
GER

Gerstein,
Mordicai.

Jonah and the two
great fish.

$16.00

YPVE54680

DATE	BORROWER'S NAME	